RADIOD

Play Along with 8 Great-Sounding Tracks

BOOK & PLAY-ALONG CDS
WITH **TNT** TONE 'N' TEMPO CHANGER

About the TNT Changer

Use the TNT software to change keys, loop playback, and mute tracks for play-along. For complete instructions, see the **TnT ReadMe.pdf** file on your enhanced CDs.

Windows users: insert a CD into your computer, double-click on My Computer, right-click on your CD drive icon, and select Explore to locate the file.

Mac users: insert a CD into your computer and double-click on the CD icon on your desktop to locate the file.

Produced by
Alfred Music Publishing Co., Inc.
P.O. Box 10003
Van Nuys, CA 91410-0003
alfred.com

Printed in USA.

ISBN-10: 0-7390-8656-1 (Book & 2 CDs)
ISBN-13: 978-0-7390-8656-8 (Book & 2 CDs)

Cover image from the original Faber Music cover by The Ghost & Stanley Donwood

Contents

2+2=5

Words and Music by
THOMAS YORKE, JONATHAN GREENWOOD,
COLIN GREENWOOD, EDWARD O'BRIEN and PHILIP SELWAY

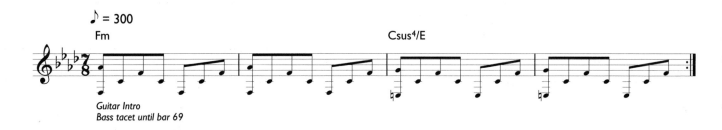

Guitar Intro
Bass tacet until bar 69

1. Are_____ you such_____ a dream_____ - ___ er? To
2. I'll_____ lay down_____ the tracks,

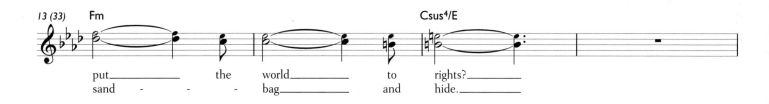

put_____ the world_____ to rights?
sand - - - bag_____ and hide._____

I'll_____ stay home for - ev - - er where
Jan - - ua - ry has A - - pril's showers and

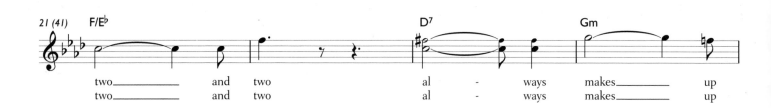

two_____ and two al - ways makes_____ up
two_____ and two al - ways makes_____ up

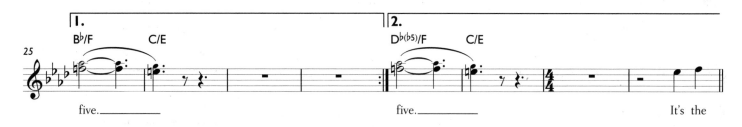

five._____
five._____ It's the

ANYONE CAN PLAY GUITAR

Words and Music by
THOMAS YORKE, JONATHAN GREENWOOD,
COLIN GREENWOOD, EDWARD O'BRIEN and PHILIP SELWAY

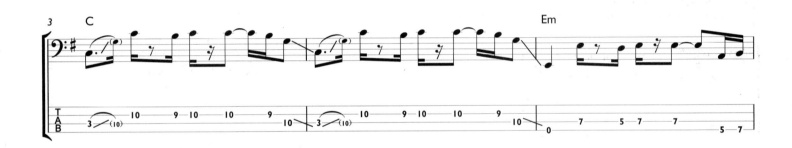

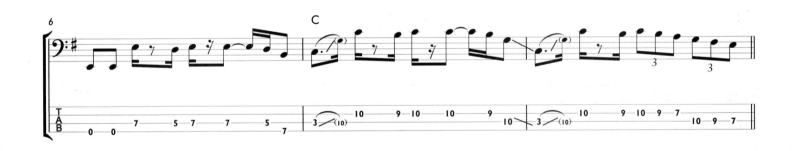

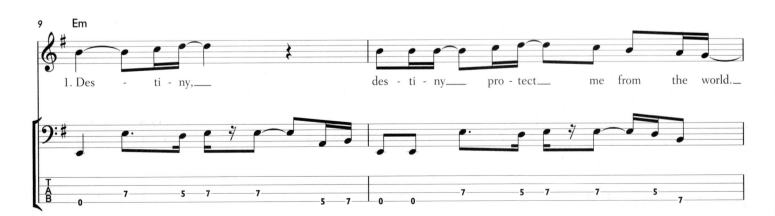

1. Des - ti - ny,___ des - ti - ny___ pro - tect___ me from the world.___

Anyone Can Play Guitar - 6 - 1

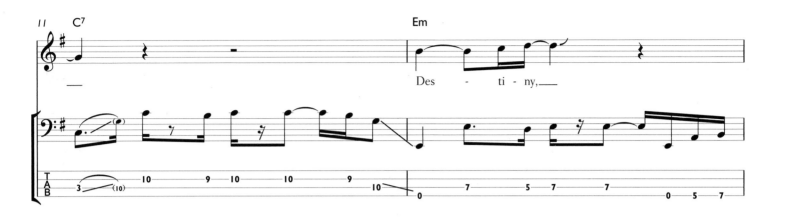

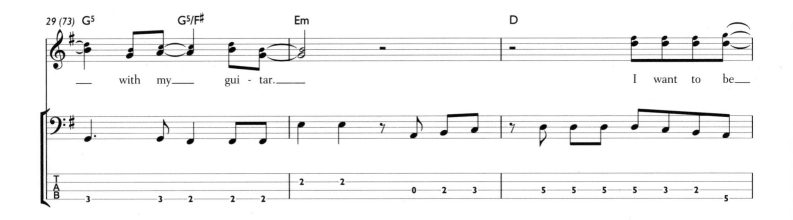

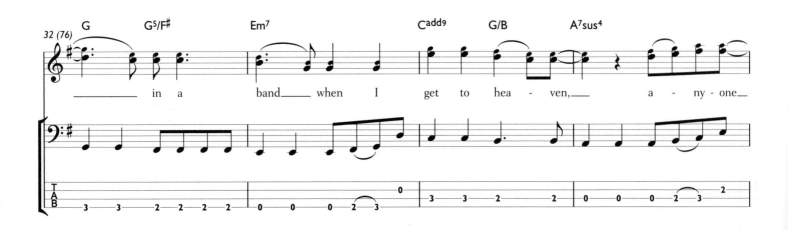

To Coda ⊕

can play gui - _tar_ and they_ won't be a no - thing a - ny - more.

tempo I ($\quad$ = 75)

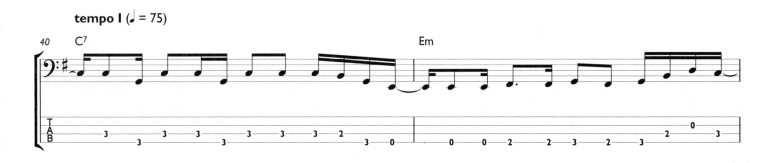

2. Grow_ my hair,_ grow my hair, I am_ Jim Mor-ri - son,_

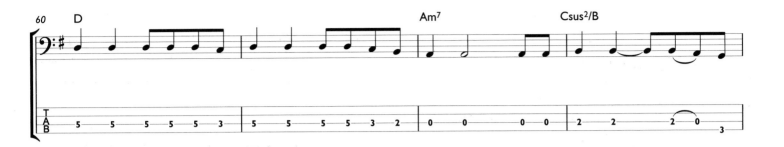

CREEP

Words and Music by
THOM YORKE, JONATHAN GREENWOOD,
PHILIP SELWAY, COLIN GREENWOOD, EDWARD O'BRIEN,
ALBERT HAMMOND and MIKE HAZELWOOD

Creep - 5 - 1

JUST

Words and Music by
THOMAS YORKE, JONATHAN GREENWOOD,
COLIN GREENWOOD, EDWARD O'BRIEN and PHILIP SELWAY

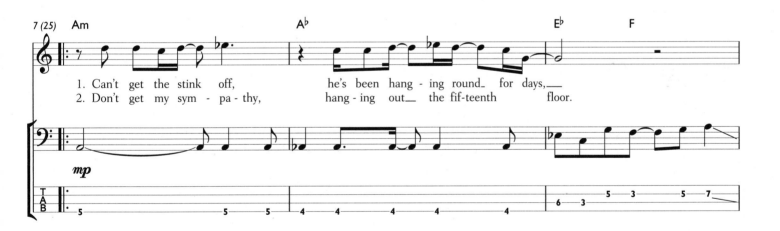

1. Can't get the stink off, he's been hang-ing round for days,
2. Don't get my sym-pa-thy, hang-ing out the fif-teenth floor.

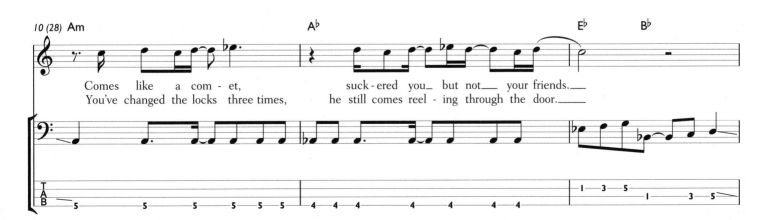

Comes like a com-et, suck-ered you but not your friends.
You've changed the locks three times, he still comes reel-ing through the door.

Just - 5 - 1

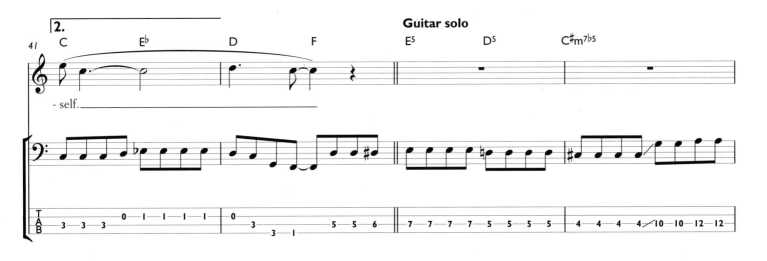

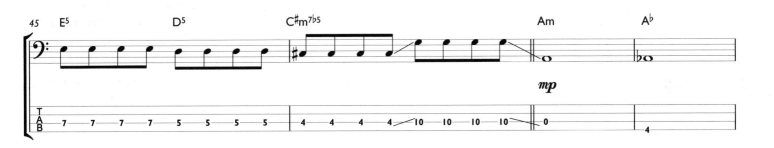

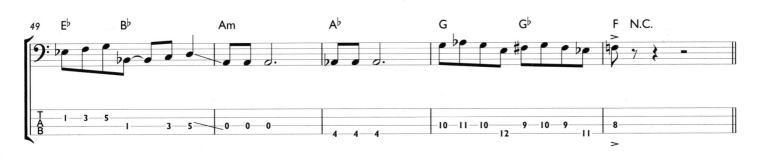

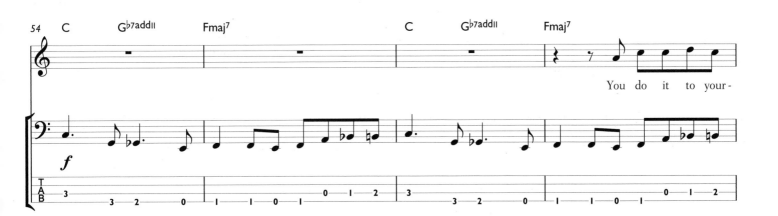

You do it to your-

KNIVES OUT

Words and Music by
THOMAS YORKE, JONATHAN GREENWOOD,
COLIN GREENWOOD, EDWARD O'BRIEN and PHILIP SELWAY

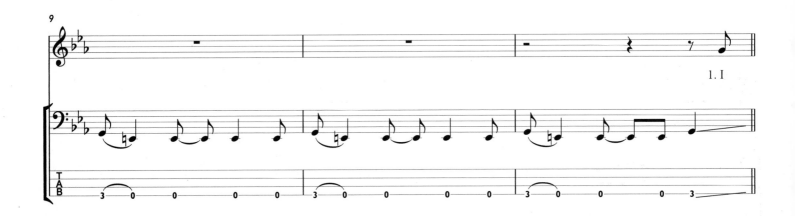

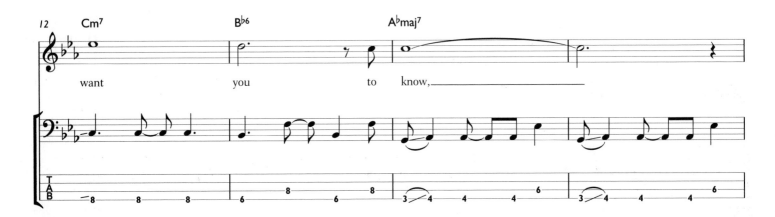

want you to know,

Knives Out - 9 - 1

Guitar solo

want you_____ to know,_____

OPTIMISTIC

Words and Music by
THOMAS YORKE, JONATHAN GREENWOOD,
COLIN GREENWOOD, EDWARD O'BRIEN and PHILIP SELWAY

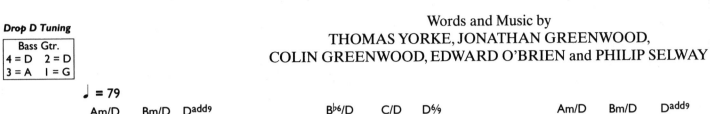

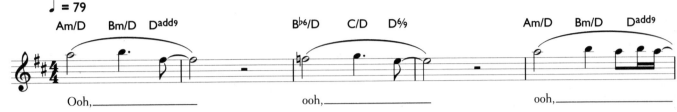

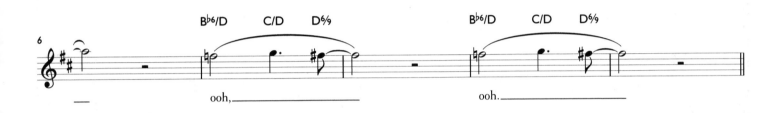

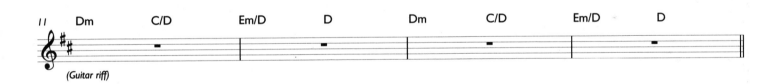

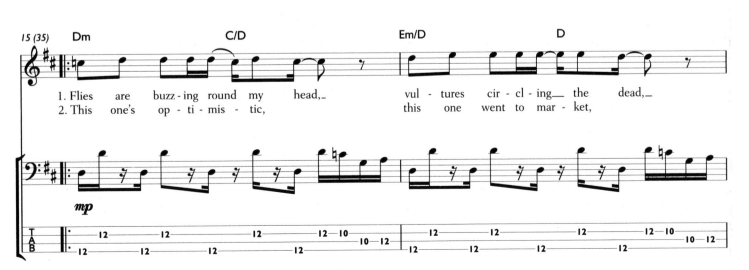

Optimistic - 8 - 1

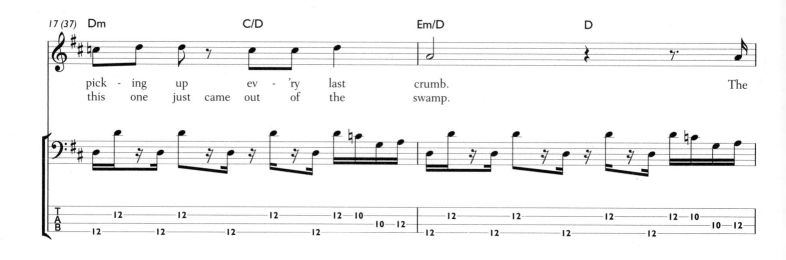

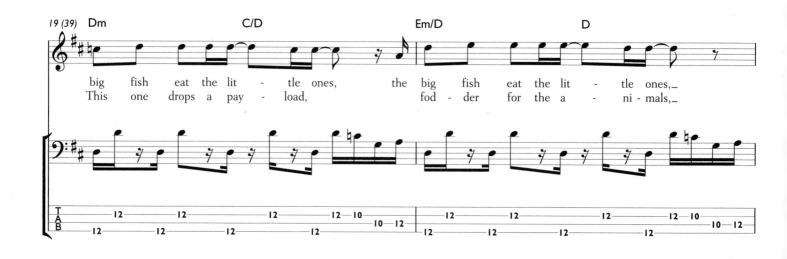

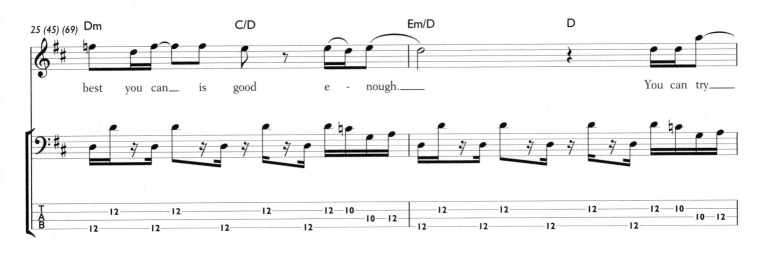

40

PARANOID ANDROID

Words and Music by
THOMAS YORKE, JONATHAN GREENWOOD,
COLIN GREENWOOD, EDWARD O'BRIEN and PHILIP SELWAY

Paranoid Android - 9 - 1

44

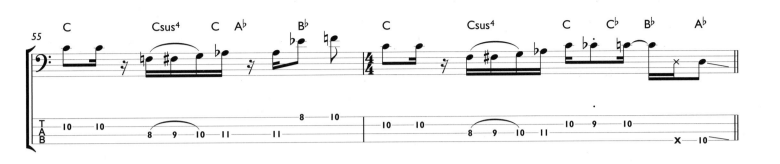

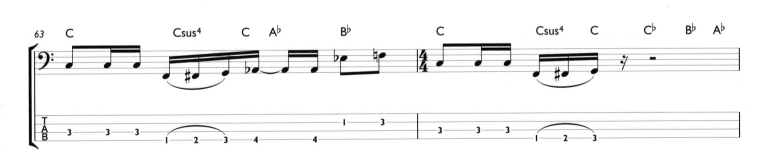

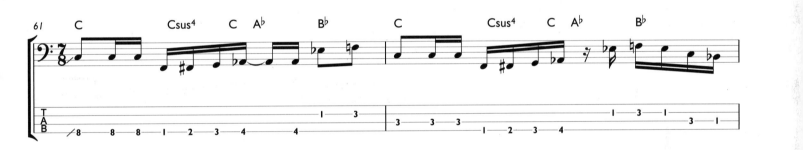

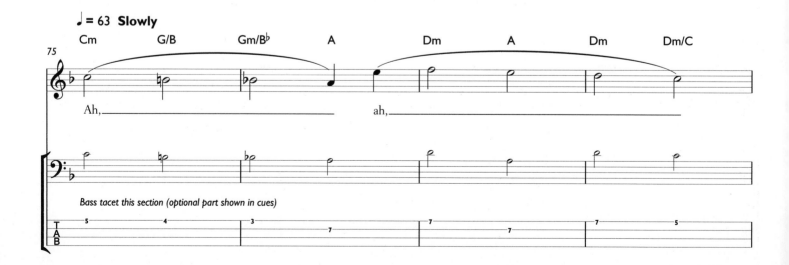

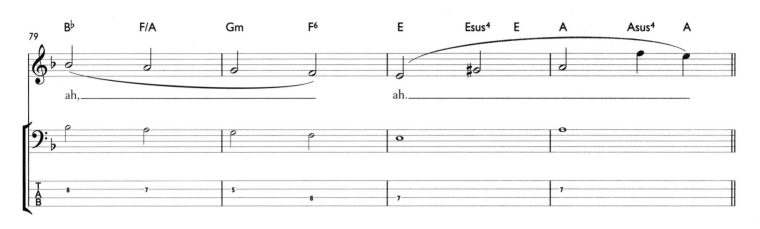

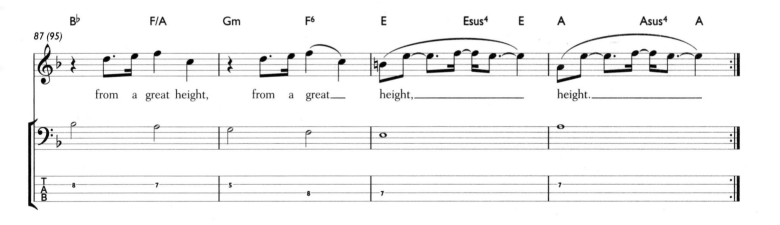

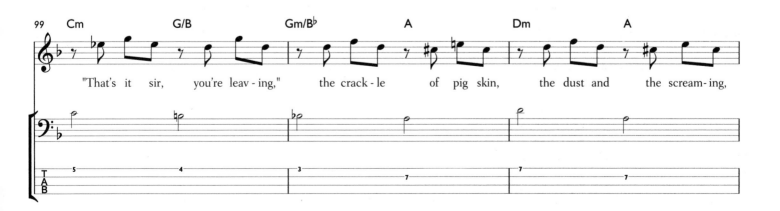

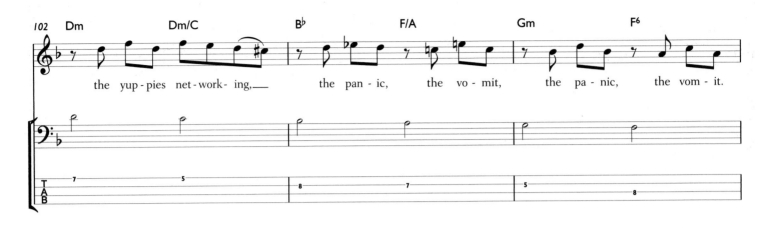

the yup - pies net - work - ing,___ the pan - ic, the vo - mit, the pa - nic, the vom - it.

God loves his child - ren, God loves his child - ren.

tempo I ♩ = 82

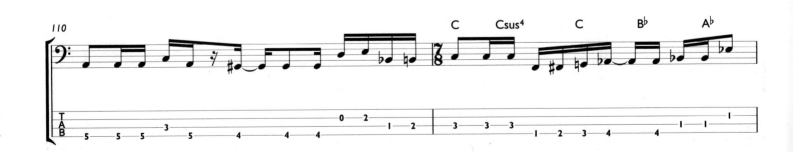

WEIRD FISHES/ARPEGGI

Words and Music by
THOMAS YORKE, JONATHAN GREENWOOD,
COLIN GREENWOOD, EDWARD O'BRIEN and PHILIP SELWAY

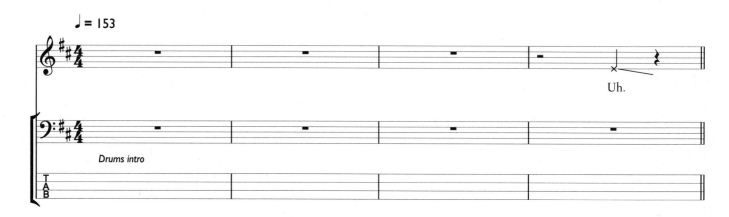

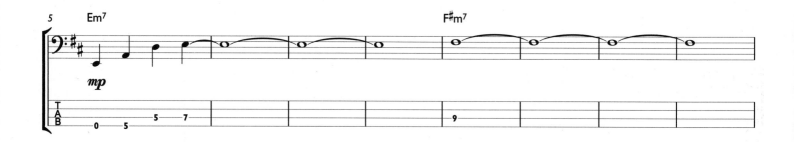

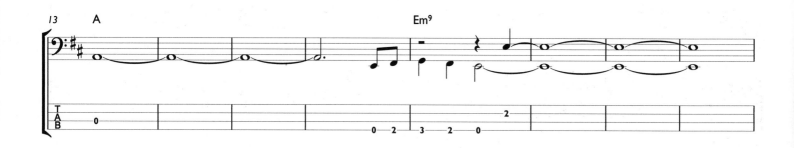

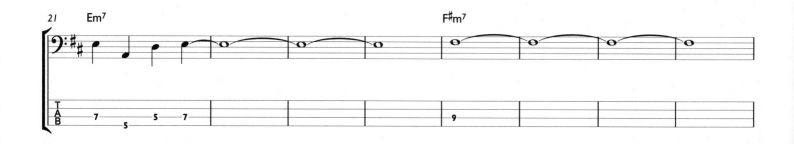

54